A PASSIONATE COMMITMENT TO ETHICAL EXPLOITATION

by Vance Boomer
Acting Chief Executive Officer

S0-ARN-537

There should be a more positive way to say this.

Who we are. Enrob is more than just the greatest multinational corporation in the history of capitalism. Enrob is a wealth-generating juggernaut fueled by a boundless synergy of courageous investors, third-world labor, reckless investment banks, and accounting practices of unmatched creativity. Thanks to our mix of pathologically aggressive management and political patronage, Enrob has devoured its competitors and will continue to do so as it diversifies into every industry on the planet.

Can't we have him smoking a cigar?

Acting CEO Vance Boomer *was appointed by Enrob directors after his predecessor, Gus Grabbitt II, was indicted for SEC violations during 2001. Vance believes that Enrob still has huge potential despite misconceived, unethical witch-hunts launched by government agencies and hypocritical consumer advocates nattering about nonexistent or picayune irregularities.*

LET'S SAY HE TOOK A LEAVE OF ABSENCE DUE TO OVERWORK.

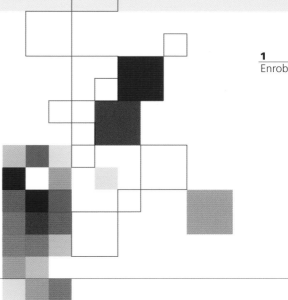

1
Enrob

What we sell. Again and again, people ask me to explain how exactly Enrob makes its money. I try to be polite when I hear this irritating question, but it's symptomatic of 1980s inside-the-box thinking that has no place in the New Economy. Enrob is a dynamic but robust innovator in resource processing and scalable connectivity, using broadband network paradigms to enrich the global data stream and minimize friction in leveraged wealth transfer models. We specialize in volatile risk assessment facilitated by an unmatched logistics skill set. What's so hard to understand about that?

ACTUALLY WE WANT TO ENHANCE THE WORLD, BUT THIS IS CLOSE ENOUGH.

Where we are going. Enrob's mission is to take over the world. To do this, everyone from New York investment bankers to little old ladies hoarding retirement nest eggs in Des Moines must be persuaded that Enrob represents a fantastic opportunity to get filthy rich. Is this a problem? Hell, no! While other upstarts in the New Economy have been compelled to admit horrendous losses, our team of forward-thinking accountants feels no such obligation. We know that nothing exceeds like excess, and "balance sheet" is an oxymoron in the New Economy. Indeed, balance is the last thing we need as we conquer markets and subject our competitors to the cutting edge of politically enabled monopoly capitalism.

Shouldn't we say, "a significant global presence"? Maybe I'm just being picky.

True, we have corporate debt—but why worry about debt, when you're shooting for global domination? Our friends in the banking industry share our optimism (they have no choice, at this point) as we demolish archaic regulations, assisted by allies in the federal government who are eager for what we have to offer. We harbor no outmoded prejudices toward one political party or the other. Where government is concerned, we're a color-blind equal-opportunity donor!

The results speak for themselves. With the Vice President of the United States, the President, and his father all playing on our team, how can we lose?

At Enrob, as always, everyone makes a bundle.

—Vance Boomer, Acting CEO

we should clarify that this is a positive attribute.

Congressman Max Greede is a stellar example of an enlightened public servant who understands that an intimate relationship between business and government benefits the whole nation. "I would be serving time for tax evasion right now if it wasn't for the influence peddlers and financial assistance I received from Enrob," Max tells us. "They can drill for oil in the Arctic Wildlife Refuge or put a hydroelectric plant in the Grand Canyon, for all I care. They'll have my vote. Of course, as a member of Congress I am absolutely in favor of term limits and campaign finance reform, if such measures become mandatory. But until then, the American people should feel secure in the knowledge that they have the best public servants that money can buy."

ENROB STOCK REBOUNDS STRONGER THAN EVER, ALMOST

During 2000 and 2001, Enrob common stock was impacted briefly by nationwide irrational pessimism disseminated by irascible losers who were jealous of the New Economy juggernaut because they had failed to climb aboard. However, our stock is exhibiting an outstandingly robust recovery, having tripled its value from $0.001 to $0.003 on the NASDAQ during early 2002. A conservative, independent think tank of independent, conservative analysts retained by Enrob has used sophisticated modeling software to affirm its independent, conservative determination that our stock is a real bargain right now. An investor purchasing $100 worth of shares will find them valued at $83,201.75 within two years if projections by our independent think tank are even in the ballpark. The message is clear. Buy Enrob stock! Buy it today! Buy a lot of it! If you earn $20,000 or more per year, you can probably afford to buy it all!

Can't we say that they just lost the documents? Maybe they had a computer problem.

We should add the usual disclaimer—you know, "this is not a formal prospectus."

Customarily, our annual reports include a balance sheet summarizing the financial status of the company. This year we have to break with tradition as a result of a regrettable error involving the shredding machine at Absolutely Honest Auditors LLC, shortly before its unfortunate federal indictment.

3
Enrob

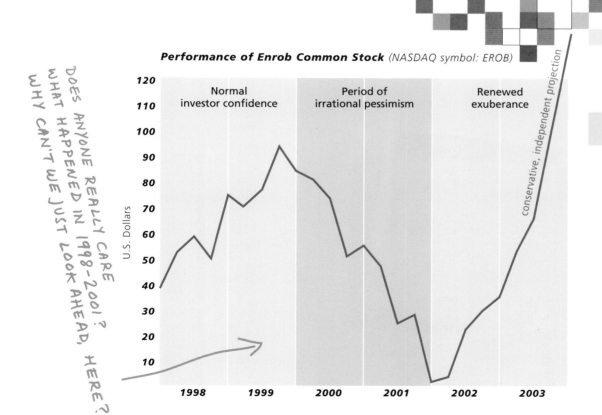

Performance of Enrob Common Stock *(NASDAQ symbol: EROB)*

Normal investor confidence	Period of irrational pessimism	Renewed exuberance

conservative, independent projection

U.S. Dollars

120
110
100
90
80
70
60
50
40
30
20
10

1998 1999 2000 2001 2002 2003

DOES ANYONE REALLY CARE WHAT HAPPENED IN 1998–2001? WHY CAN'T WE JUST LOOK AHEAD, HERE?

What a deal! *In the first quarter of 2002, Enrob shares had nowhere to go but up!*

NEAT STUFF THAT WE'LL BE MARKETING REAL SOON NOW

Human Energy Enhancement Through Smart Biotechnology. Here's a product to delight and excite managers across the entire corporate spectrum. Scientists at Enrob's biotech lab have developed "supercaff," a synthesis of stimulants to accelerate the metabolism of sluggish wage slaves, bring a buzz to their brain cells—and burn off body fat at the same time! Unmotivated laggards will experience a new zest to work longer hours with less fatigue. Result: Greater wealth for our fine nation. Supercaff uses genetically modified ingredients that are certified safe and legal, or at least they will be as soon as we complete delicate financial negotiations with senior staff at the Food and Drug Administration.

I don't like this phrase. Let's say "all natural ingredients."

Lab equipment for synthesizing Supercaff, *an energizing pick-me-up for unproductive office workers. Not recommended for pregnant women, hyperactive children, persons with a nervous disposition, or anyone who seems a high risk for running amok with semiautomatic weapons.*

This is all wrong. people are HAPPY to work in corporate America. It's a privilege!

Remote sensing in your living room! *This video receiver brings the wireless revolution to the home-office environment, displaying color images with no need for cumbersome cables or ancient phone wires. With a refresh rate of 60 hertz, the monitor offers flicker-free graphics at a surprisingly affordable price.*

THIS SHOULD READ, "FIND MUTUALLY FRUITFUL PARTNERSHIPS AMONG FELLOW VISIONARIES."

Video Without Demand. After numerous surveys, media conglomerates have concluded beyond any reasonable doubt that people who watch cable are pissed about the high monthly fee. Will they pay more to get a slightly newer movie delivered on demand? Of course not. Yet analysts and their journalistic lackeys continue to postulate that video-on-demand is the wave of the future. Since Enrob has never hesitated to jump on a New Economy bandwagon, we've established alliances with companies such as Buckbanker Video. They'll pay to access our fiber network and will pour money into it for three or four years before they realize that their Net distribution model is a nonstarter. Meanwhile, we'll be counting their cash and laughing all the way to the investment bank.

This prototype automated beverage spigot *dispenses drinks-on-demand. Designed to fill reusable cups, it eliminates the waste-disposal problems of bottles and cans. A breakthrough for environmental protection—and for Enrob!*

Automated Food and Beverage Systems. In the near future, we predict a revolution in the way that Americans eat and drink. Automated systems will cut costs, accelerate service, eliminate errors, and guarantee quality. Whether you're a fetishistic gastronome or a fast-food fanatic, you know how irritating it is when a mody food-service employee with a room temperature IQ screws up your order. At last, Enrob will take human error out of the food loop.

Electronic Money. Our research division has pioneered radical new schemes for totally secure, totally anonymous, encrypted electronic transactions. This will revolutionize online commerce while freeing consumers (and us) from the crushing burden of taxation that has ruined so many promising young companies and personal lives.

Amen to that!

Until electronic cash achieves market penetration, *our executives must rely on old-economy substitutes such as the one shown here.*

5
Enrob

HEY, I NEVER GOT MY BRIEFCASE BACK AFTER THE PHOTO SHOOT!

Don't sweat it. The photographer did relocate to Minsk, but we know where to find him.

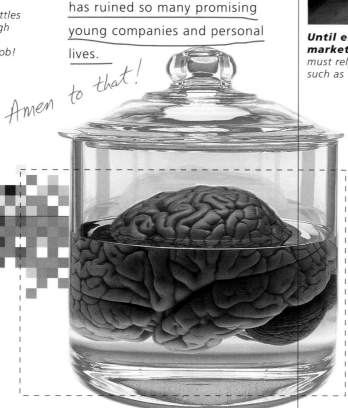

Moses Einstein, Albert Einstein's little-known younger brother, *died in 1963 but was cryogenically preserved and resuscitated at a Swiss laboratory in the mid-1990s. Today, as Chief Technology Officer (formerly deceased), he is our secret weapon in the race for new tech—truly the "brains" behind our R&D initiatives.*

Better to say it was inhibited by excessive regulation.

The Broadband Boondoggle. Rollout of high-speed internet access has slowed to a crawl, but Enrob still sees broadband as a paradigm shift comparable to the invention of fire. Why are we so pigheaded about this? Because we have a cutting-edge techno-savvy entrepreneurial vision out here on the frontiers of innovation—but mainly, we've sunk so many billions into broadband, we're stuck with it.

To save our bacon, we'll follow the same strategy that has paid off so many times before. We'll borrow more money.

During 2002 we expect to receive $1 trillion from a consortium of investment banks, gonzo dotcom gurus, Bulgarian organized crime, union pension funds, and the federal government. We'll complete hostile takeovers of Verizon, Qwest, and AT&T, at which point their old-economy obstructionism will be history. We'll dominate the entire national communications network, and we'll do whatever we want.

Broadband is yet another example of a problem that turns out to be an opportunity.

Let's say: "Bulgarian entrepreneurs."

Telecommunications— now more than ever! This rugged public-access interactive unit will enable instant data links between any two points in North America. Better still, the cost for a connection will be just a few pennies. Thanks to Enrob, tomorrow will arrive sooner than you think!

FANTASTIC! WHEN CAN I BUY ONE?

Vaporware. Enrob has studied the history of software products that are announced but never delivered, and we've concluded that this field is an exciting opportunity for any company seeking to obtain more press coverage, boost its stock valuation, and frighten competitors. Nonexistent computer applications are a natural extension of our business philosophy, and we'll be announcing several imaginary software suites in the very near future.

Sounds good but check with the legal guys.

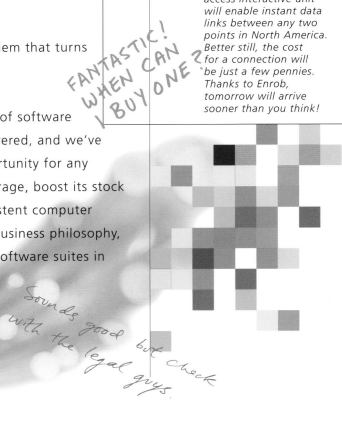

OIL AND GAS DRILLING, POWER GRIDS, PIPELINES, AND OTHER BORING STUFF

Yes, we make money by delivering oil and gas to electric companies, and we'll continue to do that. But you can't whip up investor hysteria by dealing in old-fashioned consumable resources. You need dubious new business models that depend on unproven technology that hardly anyone understands. This is why we downplay our bread-and-butter business and give maximum play to new-biz buzz.

NO, NO, NO! "CONFIDENCE," NOT "HYSTERIA"!

"Challenging" would be a much better way to phrase this.

This billion-dollar facility *generates multimegawatts with unmatched efficiency, using recycled Russian nuclear warheads as fuel. Actually we haven't built it yet, but it should be online by 2003, or 2005 if we run into any little snags.*

Ten years ago, this Peruvian hillside (below) was defaced *with unsanitary hovels. Today, it's a mine of vital resources. Enrob's strip-mining initiatives demonstrate the awesome power of political payoffs. While native elders launch lawsuits seeking compensation for supposed violations of "sacred burial grounds," Enrob is proud to say that we make our money legitimately, the old-fashioned way—by expertly engineered exploitation of the environment, not frivolous litigation.*

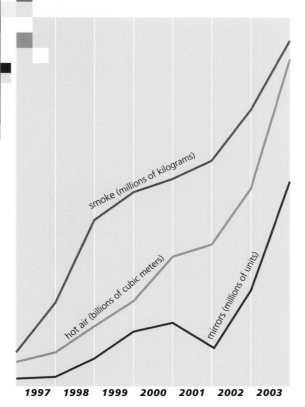

smoke (millions of kilograms)

hot air (billions of cubic meters)

mirrors (millions of units)

1997 1998 1999 2000 2001 2002 2003

Enrob has positioned itself *to be a global leader supplying manufactured goods and nonrenewable resources such as smoke, mirrors, and hot air. We're proud to be the largest U.S. supplier of these commodities to media, government, and the financial community.*

WE'RE FABRICATING A SOMEWHAT IMPLAUSIBLE FUTURE THAT WILL CHANGE YOUR LIFE, MAYBE

On Bikini atoll in the Pacific, Enrob reaps an untapped bonanza: radioactive mud from weapons tests of a bygone era. This mother lode of hot sludge is the secret ingredient powering our prototype of the world's first nuclear airplane. On a recent test flight, Geiger counters in the passenger cabin showed low levels of radiation that will actually benefit passengers by killing harmful viruses and bacteria.

Is there any way to sell radioactive stuff as a disinfectant? A cold cure? Just a thought.

Guess what—our propulsion technology is scalable! The same atomic motor that can catapult executives from New York to Shanghai before they finish sipping their first glass of Merlot will take intrepid adventurers to other planets. While NASA's cobwebbed bureaucracy tut-tuts about cost overruns afflicting its pathetic little space station, our private-enterprise colonization initiative will propel American pioneers, products, and purchasing power through interplanetary space.

It's true that we'll need a few years to iron out all the bugs in our extraterrestrial transport vehicle. But during this interim period, we won't be idle. We just picked up a bargain-basement deal on a bunch of decommissioned Titan missiles. These liquid-fueled behemoths were never designed to carry human cargo, but one dedicated Enrob employee can squeeze inside the nose cone (just about), so long as he doesn't need to wear a space suit and doesn't mind consuming his own recycled waste products. The implications are awe-inspiring. Any day now, the first private-enterprise astronaut will blast free from Earth's gravity!

WE SHOULD KEEP SPACE UNREGULATED. ARE WE WORKING ON THIS?

If there's life on Mars, do you think we can sell it anything?

The view from the backseat of our nuclear-powered stratocruiser *as it heads heavenward on a test flight from our launch facility on Bikini atoll.*

Planet Mars, a tempting target *for explorers from the private sector! Enrob's first Martian outpost will be up and running just as soon as we can borrow the money.*

In our constant quest to invade new markets *and dominate them, Enrob searches the skies. This giant communications dish in Sri Lanka scours every wave band for evidence of extraterrestrial radio transmissions. When we find an alien civilization, we'll be ready to <u>rip off anything of value that they have</u>, forge temporary alliances with their potentates, and export trashy Earth-fabricated baubles at a huge markup.*

We should say, "buy at fair market value."

Our goal? Forget about meaningless rituals such as gathering lunar rocks and saluting the flag. Profit is our purpose. Enrob's astronauts will rendezvous with asteroids rich in metal ores. We'll stake our claim on the orbital real estate and install robot machinery that will build more robot machinery. Soon, automated systems will extract thousand-ton slugs of ore and hurl them down to Planet Earth, where gigantic "catcher mitts" will field the incoming cargo. As vast refineries start cranking out carloads of extraterrestrial copper, zinc, steel, and tin, the "green zealots" who once denounced us for exploiting nonrenewable resources will be eating crow. Their angst-ridden handwringing will be history as Earth enjoys the benefits of interplanetary wealth.

HA HA!

What will it cost? We figure that $5 billion should be sufficient to export can-do capitalism into the cosmos, and we'll raise the cash from junk bonds and obscure IPOs for spinoff companies with which we will be connected in peculiar ways that we would rather not discuss right now. Investors will have a unique opportunity to reap fantastic rewards from these stock offerings that simply cannot fail to "take off"!

9
Enrob

Some of Enrob's decommissioned Titan missiles *will be converted for space exploration, but others will be restored to their original function. You read it here first: Enrob will become the first corporation in history to own intercontinental ballistic missiles with atomic warheads! Naturally we will exercise extreme restraint when deploying these terrible devices of mass destruction. But when foreign corporations use slave labor to make shoddy merchandise that they dump on the unsuspecting American consumer, judicious application of nuclear threats should make these unscrupulous opportunists reconsider their subversion of our profitability.*

I'm sick of seeing cheap Chinese imports. Can we threaten to nuke Peking, or would that violate some international treaty?

[handwritten: WHAT'S UGLY ABOUT POLITICAL INFLUENCE? I DON'T GET IT.]

THE ENROB STORY: FROM A CHEESY OLD STOREFRONT EVOLVES A MACHIAVELLIAN MEGACORP

Way back in 1993, we were just a mom-and-pop gas-heater-repair storefront in Bug Gulch, Texas. By 2001 we had become a trillion-dollar titan. How did we do it? Jealous competitors use ugly terms such as "political influence." True, we're good buddies with the President of the United States and his dad, but this is just one of those odd coincidences. We appreciate the thoughtful encouragement we've received from the executive branch, but nothing can substitute for cold cash, which is why our friends at O. K. Morebucks and SeedyCorp Global Bank are indispensable.

Begging for billions is the bedrock of our business. Mucho Benefits from Massive Borrowing is our mantra. The reason is simple: For any company that wants to achieve an insane rate of growth while bulldozing its competitors into oblivion, big-time debt is the bee's knees. Few can match our prowess at grabbing greenbacks.

[handwritten: Debt is never crippling. It is enabling!]

Many people fail to grasp the beneficial upside of crippling debt. When an upstart company rides on hype and has no coherent business plan, lenders must endorse and praise the enterprise for fear that it may go belly-up. While we service more than $1 trillion of loans, Enrob gets such good press from its banking sponsors, we're eager to borrow more. Some nervous nellies warn that we'll have to pay the piper one day, but we're too busy pursuing global domination to heed old-economy pessimism.

Who would ever imagine that a storefront in rural Texas could be the birthplace of a rapacious multinational conglomerate?

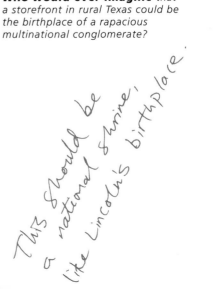

[handwritten: This should be a national shrine, like Lincoln's birthplace.]

REQUIEM FOR BUG GULCH: A POIGNANT MEMOIR

A humble shack in Bug Gulch, Texas, was the birthplace of our founder, Gus Grabbitt II. The youngest of six children, Gus dreamed of a future in which the magic of free enterprise would totally eradicate poverty (mainly, his own).

After achieving his life goals, Gus demonstrated the kinder, gentler side of capitalism when he started sending canisters of Civil Defense survival rations (past their expiration date but still edible) to his parents and siblings who still lived in the quaint old wood-framed building where Gus grew up. As he puts it, "I praise the Lord for giving me the vision to create the world's greatest corporation. But I'd trade my six mansions, my 43 servants, my 135 rare vintage cars, my fleet of yachts, my Boeing 727, my 11 mistresses, and even my hunting falcon and pet ferret for the peace of mind I used to enjoy in Bug Gulch. When I think of my folks still eking out a miserable living in that crummy little town, I have to tell you—I envy them."

Gus Grabbitt, the Father of Enrob, grew up in this humble shack. Weakened by termite infestation and decaying roof shingles, the shack collapsed during 2001, crushing all of Gus's remaining relatives. His reminiscence (left) was penned before this tragedy. We hoped he might append a memorial tribute, but at presstime he remained incommunicado while with his personal masseuse in his Bermuda vacation home, trying to come to terms with his grief.

11
Enrob

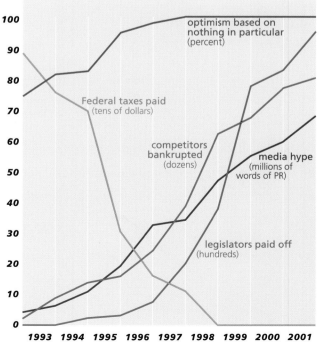

Enrob's incredible success story, told in primary indicators since the company was founded in 1993.

THE POPE OWES US A FAVOR, RIGHT? CAN WE GET HIM TO DECLARE GUS GRABBITT A SAINT?

Enrob has answered many prayers!

Right! Gus did more for the world than most saints. Well, he certainly did more for me.

What does this word mean. It doesn't sound good.

OUR UNIQUE BUSINESS MODEL BENEFITS SOCIETY, EVISCERATES COMPETITORS, AND RAKES IN HUGE PILES OF CASH

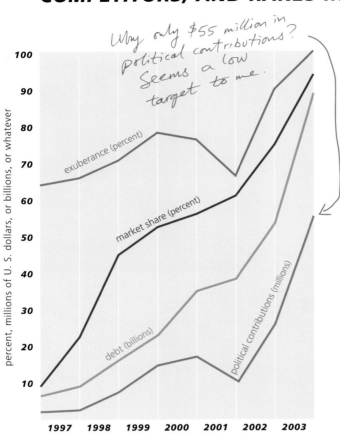

Why only $55 million in political contributions? Seems a low target to me.

All our leading indicators *are trending up, up, and away! (Figures for 2002 and 2003 based on reliable guesses by our in-house team of conservative, independent analysts.)*

While we've been portrayed as advocates of the free market, this is not entirely accurate. A completely free market drives down prices and pares profits to the bone, tempting companies to sell shoddy, cut-rate merchandise. This self-defeating strategy threatens their own survival and damages patriotic public trust in American capitalism as we know it.

The business model offering maximum benefits to society and our shareholders (and us) is commonly known as a state-sanctioned monopoly. Theoretically the Justice Department opposes this, but in practice it intervenes mainly in cases in which a corporation such as Microsoft is too arrogant to pay protection money. At Enrob, we never make that mistake. As major-league donors to political campaigns and the White House, we enjoy thinly veiled groveling from legislators, enabling us to dominate most markets without fear of inconveniences such as antitrust action.

Having established a monopoly, our next step is to set price points that will minimize our risk and achieve healthy profitability. By eliminating fickle consumer choice, we are better positioned to bankroll our vision of distributing gifts of technology to disadvantaged nations in every corner of the world.

In the short term, consumers who fail to understand this vision may accuse us of transgressions such as "gouging." Rather than engage our opponents in a pointless debate, we prefer to blame energy price fluctuations on OPEC and the Arabs. Here again we enjoy assistance from the federal government, which has a long tradition of demonizing Middle Eastern nations—except for Israel, of course.

I do so wish we could educate more people about this.

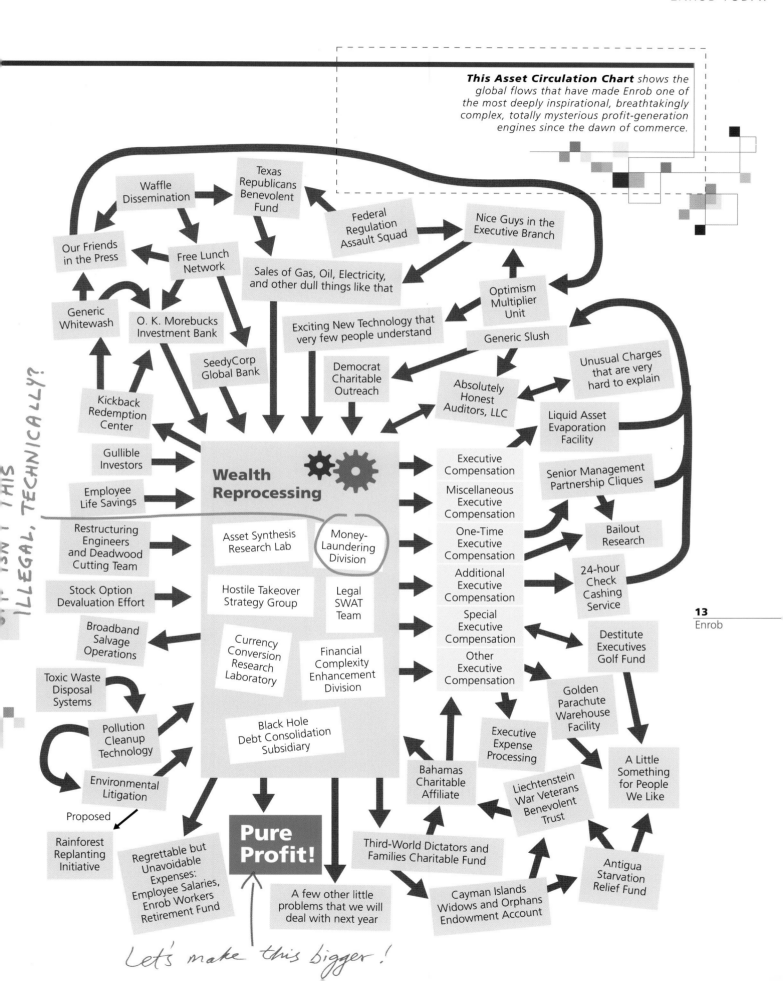

*This **Asset Circulation Chart** shows the global flows that have made Enrob one of the most deeply inspirational, breathtakingly complex, totally mysterious profit-generation engines since the dawn of commerce.*

COPING STRATEGIES IN A CASH-STRAPPED BUSINESS ENVIRONMENT

Once in a while, our great nation's inexorable climb toward the pinnacle of infinite wealth is interrupted by a minority of bumbling bureaucrats whose understanding of commerce is poor at best. These public-sector meddlers should know by now that it hurts them as much as it hurts us when they bite the "invisible hand" of capitalism that feeds them. Still, government-triggered economic downturns are a fact of life, and Enrob knows from grim experience that at times like these, suppliers beg for more generous terms and may even try to weasel out of deals. Meanwhile, resellers and retailers adopt a "can't pay, won't pay" attitude that has no place in a free economy.

The whiners and wheedlers seem to forget that in a recession our corporation is threatened like any other. Consequently, our priority is to screw money out of debtors and enforce (ruinous) contractual terms on our suppliers with even more fanatical zeal than usual. We have zero tolerance for pathetic attempts to plead poverty. Our position is simply summarized: All resellers and retailers are crooks—because they have OUR MONEY!

When a debtor visited our offices to discuss his repayment schedule, Vice President for Fiduciary Compliance Janey Wallop discovered that he was a little less cash-strapped than he had led her to believe.

At the dinner table in Enrob's executive suite, component supplier Timothy Welsh finds himself confronted with a giant helping of lightly steamed broccoli. As Welsh recoils in horror from his worst culinary phobia, he realizes we're ready to play hardball. Soon after this picture was taken, Welsh acquiesced to some new, stringent contractual conditions.

I hate that we have to pay them off just to get them to leave us alone. The feds are worse than the Mafia. At least the Mafioso guys are honest about what they do!

Right!

NOT "RUINOUS." THE TERMS ARE "FAIR."

any police interrogator knows, force should be
[int]erspersed judiciously with unexpected acts of
[compas]ion. Nelson Groat, CEO of our largest power
[s]eller on the West Coast, was moved to tears when an
[En]rob representative proffered a raspberry-flavored
[lol]ipop to Groat's son Boris. Two days later, we were not
[sur]prised when Groat sent a check for the full
[$]50,302,001.29 that he owed.

**What to do, when bribery, negotiation, and
legal threats all fail** to get results? Enrob passes its
worst delinquent accounts to Beltolli and Filch, the
notorious debt collection agency in Las Vegas. When
Bob Beltolli's bullyboys pay an unexpected call,
deadbeat debtors sometimes take pathetically desperate
measures to defend themselves. Sooner or later,
though, they face facts, knuckle under, and do what
they should have done all along: open their wallets.

*Janey Wallop, our Vice President for
Fiduciary Compliance,* has added a rich variety of
enforcement tactics to Enrob's arsenal of strategies
in the Department of Revenue Extraction. So far as
Janey is concerned, lawsuits are for pussies. If
deadbeats owe cash, she goes for the throat—or any
other exposed part of the anatomy.

[handwritten] IT SHOULD BE A CRIMINAL ACT WHEN PEOPLE ARE LATE IN PAYING US. CAN WE GET A LAW PASSED?

**Enrob's Vice President for Investor
Liaison Ling Yi Yang** *knows how to
lubricate relationships with business partners
and clients, when necessary. Former COO
Jackson J. Jackson discovered Ling's talents
when she made a surprise appearance at an
interest-rate-reduction office party at the
Federal Reserve in July 2001.*

15
Enrob

[handwritten] Let's not say "bribery." We apply "incentives."

ENROB PAYS TRIBUTE TO FRIENDS IN HIGH PLACES, LOW PLACES, OR WHEREVER—WE'RE NOT FUSSY

(handwritten note in left margin:) We understand that government doesn't work. Not unless we give it some "help"!

(handwritten note in lower left margin:) HEY, THE WORD IS "DONATIONS," NOT "GRAFT." PLEASE!

The biggest secret to Enrob's success? We understand how government works. From two-bit island republics to ruthless communist regimes . . . from the nepotism of Arab emirates to the corruption of so-called Western democracies . . . we have learned that all politicians share a similar need. They need money! And we're happy to give it to them—so long as they understand the meaning of "quid pro quo." Enrob is not a charitable institution; everyone should understand that graft is a win-win proposition.

We'd like you to meet all of our wholly owned functionaries, but there are thousands of them, and many prefer to remain anonymous. Here are just a few who have assisted Enrob in its patriotic mission to kick aside regulatory roadblocks and give consumers everything they want at a price they can barely afford.

Viewed here through a typical London fog, *Her Majesty Queen Elizabeth II praises Enrob's financial acumen: "I really appreciated the generous donation that we received from those nice young men at Enrob after we put a word in for them at the Bank of England. Their unexpected gift will enable us to turn up the thermostat at Balmoral Castle from 55 to 60 degrees next winter, and we can buy three new litters of fox hounds."*

Turning Effluence into Affluence. City Councillor Ruby Rich of Oklahoma is a woman whose unique vision is exceeded only by her deep appreciation for money. When we helped Ruby in her reelection campaign, she returned the favor by backing our plan to install fiber-optic communications via municipal sewer pipes. After specially trained rats ran through the pipes with nylon threads tied to their tails, engineers used the threads to drag fishing line, and the fishing line dragged fiber. Today, Okies have Ruby to thank when they enjoy the luxury of web surfing while sitting on the toilet. Without her vision and her willingness to be paid off, data distribution via sewer networks would still be just a dream.

One of the team of trained rats *that brought high-speed data transfer to bathrooms all over Oklahoma.*

Finally, a Practical Use for Endangered Species.

In a noble effort to reduce Japan's dependence on energy imports, Governor Oyako Donburi of the Kujira Prefecture endorsed our mission to establish the world's first power facility that burns whale oil. When anxious advocates of Japan's ailing whale-killing industry were told of this timely initiative, they exclaimed, "Arigato, Enrob!"

When Enrob's Bahamaian banking enterprise

learned that auditors were planning a surprise visit, one person leaped to our aid: Senator Ava Rice of Nevada. "Guns don't kill people, people kill people," Ms. Rice explains succinctly. "It's the same with money. Money doesn't commit crimes. There's no such thing as dirty money, so who gives a hoot about laundering it? When Enrob asked me to run $10 billion in cash through a few casinos, I said sure—so long as I got my end."

Governor Oyako Donburi of the Kujira Prefecture enjoys the karmic heft of a bag of bullion donated by Enrob in appreciation for her support for our initiative to turn dead whales into valuable electricity. "Environmentalists say whales so smart, are sacred species," Ms. Donburi comments. "I say whales should feel honored to sacrifice lives for noble Japanese people. Dead whales may be reincarnated as environmentalists, hah-hah. Thank you, Enrob, for processing valuable whale oil to burn in Japanese generator furnaces."

17
Enrob

Senator Ava Rice of Nevada, wearing a necklace of gold-plated gambling chips awarded to her by Enrob in appreciation for her tireless dedication to money laundering.

I have never understood the concept of money laundering.

The Feds invented it. It's supposed to stop businesses from making a cash profit and not paying taxes.

HA!

ENROB'S EMISSARIES WORK TIRELESSLY TO GREASE WHEELS AND PALMS IN GOVERNMENT

WHEN DID THEY LET HIM OUT OF SAN QUENTIN?

For our chief Washington lobbyist, *invisibility is a priceless asset. Like a cross between Santa Claus and a Stealth jet, he moves silently, often at night, and leaves no trace as he delivers legislative incentive packages.*

That's a good way to express the concept

Acting Senior Vice President for the North American Tactical Squad, *John Doe (not his real name) has developed innovative techniques to enlighten a small minority of stubborn legislators who have been reluctant to embrace our vision of state-assisted, not-entirely-free-market capitalism.*

FINE NEW FACILITIES WILL SATISFY ENROB'S INSATIABLE GROWTH, SOMETIME FAIRLY SOON PROBABLY

We think our headquarters *in Los Angeles will look like this after we build it.*

Enrob's future home in Washington, D.C., *currently occupied by tenants who have ceased cooperating with us. Eviction is expected within the next two years.*

Or sooner, if you don't shape up, George, old Pal!

Where better to install *a corporation that pays lip service to total market freedom? The interior of this well-known statue is mostly empty, but will contain Enrob executive offices as soon as we conclude financial arrangements with appropriate government functionaries.*

ENROB DUMPS DEADBEATS, LEVERAGES LIQUIDITY, PUMPS PROFITS!

Our corporation is more than just a maniacal global enterprise, it's a community that has been built by special, dedicated people with irreplacable skills. We see our employees as a glorious extended family.

Right, it's a family and we're the parents. So how come we don't get more respect?

Unfortunately, some of these family members tend to get complacent and lazy. We would not be doing our duty to stockholders if we allowed this tendency to persist unchecked. The core strength of Enrob would be threatened. Consequently, restructuring has been a key goal at Enrob.

During 2001, Joe Swathe, Vice President for Corporate Downsizing, led Project Deadwood, which culled an amazing 25,675 unnecessary employees worldwide and developed revolutionary accounting methods to devalue stock options while eliminating costly pension plans. This saved us billions and strengthened Enrob in its mission to serve humanity. Thanks, Joe!

Typical response of an Enrob employee *when Mr. Swathe's bulky figure looms in the doorway of an office cubicle.*

Joe Swathe, *Vice President for Corporate Downsizing*

WAY TO GO, JOE! DOWNSIZE THOSE DRONES!

Tell his Holiness that if he doesn't come through for us, we'll repossess his bulletproof limo.

ALMOST ALWAYS—TOTALLY ETHICAL

IS THIS REALLY TRUE?

We play by our rules. Enrob has never knowingly violated any state or federal regulations. Why should we, when we can pay legislators to rewrite laws that get in the way? True, our accounting procedures are so complex, even our senior managers don't understand them all. However, our confederates at Absolutely Honest Auditors, LLC, are eternally vigilant. In the unlikely event that they discover we have cut a few corners here and there, undoubtedly it was a good-faith attempt to enhance public perception of our company and inflate its valuation for the benefit of our stockholders (and us). As always, our accounting staff are the investor's best friends.

maybe not. But who's counting?

This coveted Medal of Peace *is issued only to exceptional visionaries who are judged worthy by the Vatican. No one at Enrob has received this award yet, but after our recent donation to the Pope, we feel confident that our prayers will be answered.*

Inspirational Wealth Enhancement. Enrob is a pioneer in the field of unregulated, tax-exempt virtual future energy derivatives, sometimes known as UNFEDs. This little-known quasifinancial bearer instrument was engineered by a brilliant innovator with impeccable ethical credentials: Sister Angelica, a former nun who became an SEC regulator and now serves as our chief financial officer. UNFEDs will double our net profit in FY 2002 (before special charges against earnings, in theory, on paper, using the triple-compounded depreciation model, not including undeclared long-term debt and political slush funds currently under investigation by the General Accounting Office).

Sister Angelica *looks for guidance in a volume of the Internal Revenue Service Corporate Tax Code.*

Acting Vice President for Internal Affairs *Jack Sargeant is relentless in his determination to ensure that Enrob conforms with all standard business practices, except those which we feel are onerous, inconvenient, or unreasonable.*

EFFECTIVE COMMUNICATION: HELPING UNENLIGHTENED PEOPLE TO SEE THINGS OUR WAY

Vice President for Public Affairs *Polly Snitch will say hello to just about anyone.*

Industry Analysts: Our Best Buddies (next to bankers).
Some of our unethical competitors have smeared Enrob as a cut-throat cabal of aggressive maniacs who pay off politicians everywhere from New Zealand to Zaire. What can we do when jealous detractors circulate unfounded innuendo? We use world-class PR to put a positive spin on it.

At Enrob, free lunches are just the first taste of our
smorgasboard of treats for "industry analysts" who pontificate in business journals and on TV. As for regular journalists—anyone who says that you can't buy good press can't have tried very hard. While honest reporters can't be bribed, there are so few of them, fortunately for us, they can be safely ignored.

To some people, "hype" is a dirty word.
At Enrob we see it as a valuable tool for setting goals and motivating our workforce. Being modest and self-effacing is a path to corporate suicide.

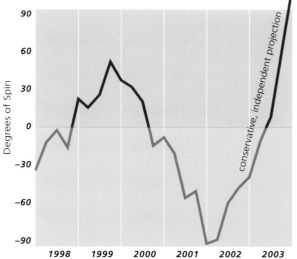

conservative, independent projection

Degrees of Spin: 90, 60, 30, 0, -30, -60, -90 — 1998 1999 2000 2001 2002 2003

21
Enrob

This spin graph compiled by Enrob's PR division *measures our depiction in the left-leaning, anticapitalist, totally untrustworthy American media.*

Vice President for Equal Opportunity Outreach *Hortense Washington deals promptly and effectively with any misguided, money-motivated complaints of racial bias in Enrob's hiring practices.*

Personally I resent the money we spend on PR. If some people are so dumb, they don't understand our contribution to global prosperity thats their problem.

BUILDING AN INTIMIDATING, UNAVOIDABLE INTERNATIONAL PRESENCE

SOMETIMES I WONDER IF THIS GUY IS REALLY A TEAM PLAYER.

At Enrob, we will not rest until the benefits of our amazingly wonderful corporate enterprise are enjoyed not only in Beverly Hills mansions but in the humblest third-world shantytown. Unfortunately, in many small nations everyone from El Presidente to the local lawman is on the take, and if you don't grease their palms, there's no way they'll let you flatten a few refugee camps to make room for productive oil wells or a fine new dam.

We face a terrible dilemma. Should we abandon the local citizens to their lives of miserable deprivation, or enhance the local economy by paying off the bully-boys, so that we can flood some valleys and grab nonrenewable resources? Our conclusion is clear: The needs of the people outweigh any qualms we might have about political corruption. This is especially true since each dollar we donate to despots eventually trickles down to those in need.

Do you think anyone will really believe this?

Senior Vice President for International Graft
Salaam Hindi, pictured here in his mountain retreat, offers financial assistance to kings, dictators, and other nabobs whose shortsighted self-interest threatens to throttle third-world commerce. Just as GIs gave candy bars to oppressed Europeans during World War II, Enrob dispenses a highly prized American commodity among the international ruling class: money!

Enrob's "power for dollars" *international initiative will enrich our senior management while creating opportunities for millions of parents and children who are electrically impaired. The droning hum of high-voltage lines will be a constant reminder that at Enrob, we care.*

You know, the drains smell bad and the roof leaks?

Enrob's future British headquarters lacks modern plumbing and other amenities but is scheduled for occupation after renovation.

The Enrob building in India. *We expect to take possession after installing necessary communications dishes and antennas on the roof.*

The Enrob headquarters in Japan, *which we hope to buy after we do our part to trash the value of the yen.*

At Enrob, selfless duty to our corporate dream is a daily reality. *Our executives and directors endure disorienting jet lag, traumatic culture shock, extreme temperatures, and bowel-loosening local food in their dedication to cut deals in every corner of the world. From the depressing isolation of the Hawaiian islands to the arid, oven-hot beaches of the Caribbean, we go where duty calls, regardless of personal discomfort.*

These old buildings are overrated. most of them are falling apart. I say we forget about trying to buy "class" and build something new and ugly and comfortable.

NOT TO MENTION THE EXCRUCIATING PAIN OF SUNBURN!

INTERNATIONAL ESPIONAGE: A NEW WEAPON IN OUR CORPORATE ARSENAL

We learned long ago that the free market is a battlefield, and business is war. This explains our strategic decision to establish a rapport with the Central Intelligence Agency. When CIA assets slip us the scoop on third-world despots, we make discreet deposits in the spooks' Liechtenstein bank accounts, and everyone ends up smiling.

CIA spies tell us valuable tidbits about overseas dictators and warlords, such as their favorite Western rock bands, their wives' preferences in jewelry and house furnishings, and their weapons of choice for maiming seditious antigovernment rebels. Empowered with this privileged information, our emissaries visit an emperor's mountain fortress or a colonel's bamboo hut with gifts of gold-plated flatware, Britney Spears CDs, and appropriate video clips from international arms dealers. Result: A massive inflow of foreign currency from sultans, sheiks, potentates, and others with a need for our unique corporate services.

Regrettably, some banana-republic generalissimos are eager to do business but lack the muscle to quell dissident factions. Purely in the interests of furthering global commerce, Enrob has devised a special program to help them. We maintain a discreet and unofficial understanding with Colonel Fritz "Mad Eagle" Mallet, whose French aristocratic heritage extends back to Napoleon (his family name is pronounced "mallay"). "Mallet's Mashers," consisting of two platoons of hardened mercenaries, are constantly ready to be airlifted to any trouble spot where collectivists, Moslem extremists, or ignorant peasants waving pitchforks threaten to disrupt the orderly processes of government and free enterprise.

The great visionary of Pago Largo, Emperor Bobo Mahoud, receives 500 billion zlotys from Enrob's Distressed Despot Account in appreciation for his help in a massive project to turn extinct volcanoes into nuclear waste repositories. When the Emperor needed a multinational giant with the experience to move dirt, bend rebar, pour concrete, and airdrop drums of deadly radioactive detritus into the gaping maw of volcanic cinder cones, Enrob was there. We don't know why the Emperor preferred Polish currency for his payoff, or where he stashed the loot, and we don't care. All we know is that this fine engineering project has leveraged Pago Largo into the twenty-first century, and Enrob made a bundle out of it. The Emperor chose to accept his check in front of the Tomb of the Unknown Pirate on the undisclosed Bahamaian island where Enrob's international banking center is located.

ARE YOU SURE WE WANT TO GO PUBLIC WITH THIS?

No problem. The guys at CIA have signed an exclusive 5-year contract.

What is their problem?

Incredible! These guys just never seem to quit!

Enrob doesn't underestimate its opponents.
Scurrilous propaganda still deludes naive hotheads into imagining that wealth should be shared in conformance with the Communist model. Even more dangerous are Moslem fanatics who characterize our fine nation as a rapacious, power-crazed brute that exploits and oppresses its weaker neighbors. The truth, of course, is that Enrob pays fair market value for all the resources that we plunder, and our paramilitary associates subjugate local guerrillas only when they threaten the liberty that is sacred to us in the Free World.

Using friendly persuasion (or unfriendly persuasion where necessary), Enrob works to convince even the most muddle-headed Marxist that capitalism is everyone's best bet—not just for generating wealth, but for distributing it to those who deserve it most, such as brilliant visionaries who create corporations that will change the world.

Hong Wai Bun, a dedicated member of Colonel Fritz "Mad Eagle" Mallet's commando unit, *displays the tools of her trade in a jungle near the Cambodian border. Until "Mallet's Mashers" stepped in, strongman Ho Lee Fok was fighting a losing battle to build a vital nuclear reactor and plutonium-reprocessing facility. Contrary to the scaremongering of local Marxist fanatics, this installation will electrify local villages while enriching tribal elders by employing them as plant supervisors. Thanks to Enrob, for the first time in their lives they'll enjoy sufficient wealth to drink Coke, wear Levi's, and watch MTV relayed via a microwave link from Enrob's communications center in Saigon.*

25
Enrob

Colonel Fritz "Mad Eagle" Mallet *is a renaissance man whose diverse hobbies include archery, vivisection, and playing Bach preludes on a dulcimer strung with the intestines of his defeated enemies.*

FINALLY, THE TRUTH ABOUT JUNGLES! NOW, IF ONLY PEOPLE WOULD LISTEN.

ENLIGHTENED CAPITALISM—THE ENVIRONMENT'S BEST FRIEND

Let the sun shine in! *Unsightly, unsanitary trees are cleared by an Enrob bulldozer equipped with "monster claw."*

Global warming is not a problem. It is a fantastic business opportunity.

Myth: Rain forests enhance the global environment.

Fact: Impenetrable vegetation is infested with poisonous vermin and nightmarish diseases. Sprawling nests of noxious, rotting plants function like giant compost heaps, fouling the atmosphere with greenhouse gases that worsen global warming. Our duty is obvious: Enhance the ecosphere by ripping evil-smelling jungles off the face of the earth, thus opening valuable land for shopping malls, tract homes, and parking lots.

Alternative Energy Sources. Enrob has little interest in alternative energy sources such as windmills and solar panels, since we can't figure out a way to make much money out of them. Still, if any of these half-baked ideas turns out to be profitable, we'll file patents, sue our competitors, and nail them to the wall.

Short-Term Solution: No Sweat! Enrob plans a huge initiative to address the problem of global warming. First, we will build 25,000 miles of pipeline around the globe (see photo). Next, we'll pump 5 trillion barrels per year of ice slush from the Arctic and Antarctic to equatorial nations such as Africa and South America, where excessive heat reduces productivity while making people bad tempered and giving them headaches. This engineering feat, backed with pledges from fifteen governments, the UN, the World Bank, the European Community, Fort Knox, the British Royal Family, and OPEC, with special exemptions from the IRS, should be up and running by the first quarter of 2004, or maybe 2005 if some of our sponsors begin to experience "hype fatigue."

Can we not mention the IRS? Makes me nervous. Just an irrational kind of thing.

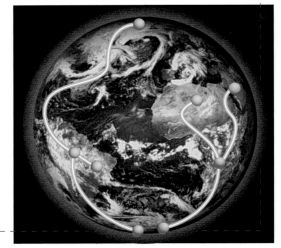

Enrob's global pipeline, *currently under tentative preliminary discussion prior to hypothetical modeling, will help Planet Earth to beat the heat.*

Eighteen billion barrels seems a bit low. Can we revise this estimate upward, if you catch my drift?

Conservation—of Oil, Gas, and Money!

Although Enrob has been accused of marketing energy products that spew greenhouse gases into the upper atmosphere, the truth is, we hate energy hogs. We'll discourage their wanton waste in the one way that works: by whacking them in the wallet. When we double or triple the price of oil, gas, and electricity (with a little help from our friends in Washington), demand will level off faster than you can say "Kyoto Agreement." During the California energy crisis we already proved that reducing the supply while conspiring with regulators to jack up the price created a net gain for us—and the environment too, of course.

Toxic waste generated by Enrob facilities worldwide.

Billions of barrels

22
21
20
19
18
17
16
15
14
13
12
11
10
9
8
7
6
5
4
3
2
1

1997 1998 1999 2000 2001

Toxic waste cleanup technology promises to generate a massive revenue stream for Enrob as communities and municipalities address unintended consequences of our previous activities.

Toxic Waste Yields Lucrative Payoffs.

Like any huge corporation that deals with dangerous chemicals, Enrob has its share of catastrophic accidents—and we're ready to make money out of them. When one of our gas pipelines caught fire in Dubai, it deposited evil-smelling soot over several historic mosques, two schools, a hospital, and several thousand hovels. We responded aggressively by developing and deploying Sludgeaway, our patented macrodetergent cleaner. When the cleaner contaminated local aquifers, our scientists created Scaldit, a steam-injection system that literally blasts pollution out of the ground. When this system malfunctioned and poisoned water holes over an area of 90 square miles, killing several thousand elephants, we countered with an even more revolutionary product. Named Bactrobeam, it disperses pollution-eating bacteria by using massive lasers originally developed for the Strategic Defensive Initiative.

At this time we make no representation that the lasers will be totally safe for insects, endangered bird species, and operating personnel, but as engineers with a conscience, we remain committed to our motto: "We'll keep doing it till we get it right."

So long as people keep paying us, of course. Should we mention that?

27
Enrob

SOUR LOSERS AND SOREHEADS TRASH A CORPORATE CORNUCOPIA

Late in 2001, Enrob suffered a severe setback when a trusted high-ranking employee turned out to be an obsessive delusional psycho whose pathology induced him to attack the entity that had rewarded him so generously over the years. When he circulated baseless allegations against higher management, to our amazement he was revered as a "whistleblower" in the popular press. Some journalists were evidently prejudiced against our company, probably because they failed to buy Enrob stock when we advised them to do so, or failed to sell it at the optimal price point. Senators whom we had considered our trusted friends then pandered to mob hysteria and ruined the careers of our finest servants by tarnishing their reputations with vile innuendo.

THAT MISERABLE FINK! AND PEOPLE SAY THAT WE LACK INTEGRITY!

Those scum-sucking weasels! We deserve a refund!

Our seven new directors, *ready to serve our company and pursue its mission of excellence.*

UGLY FALLOUT FROM HYPOCRITICAL "REFORMERS"

This has to be the greatest tragedy in the history of world commerce. Is there no justice?

Since Enrob is committed to the highest standards of integrity, its accused officers and directors voluntarily stepped down. Each was awarded a modest $100 million severance package and a year's salary, sufficient to seek work elsewhere as industry consultants or in government agencies. A new interim team has taken their place (see photos, opposite). While circumstances have forced us to make hasty appointments, stockholders can feel confident that our acting officers and directors will uphold Enrob's highest ethical traditions.

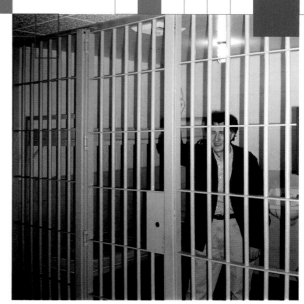

As shown in this news photo, our Chief Financial Officer *Buck Moore endured the humiliation of being treated like a common criminal. If Buck is allowed a decent opportunity to refute allegations of fraud, insider trading, stock manipulation, racketeering, and passing bad checks at his local 7-Eleven, we have no doubt that he will regain his rightful status as a financial genius who enriched modern civilization.*

Not at the Justice Department, that's for sure. They act as if we never paid them anything.

Attacks on Enrob during 2001 were not just a jealous tantrum from whiners who resented our triumphs. They were a heretical renunciation of faith in the free-enterprise system—an un-American body blow against gung-ho entrepreneurs worldwide. For shame!

The unprincipled creeps who rocked Enrob with a volley of baseless allegations became overnight media whores, with book deals to follow. They did well for themselves, but at whose expense? The pain was most intense among the gifted leaders who crafted Enrob's empire, but it didn't end there. Legitimate businesses were dragged down as they lost the generosity of those who used to throw around huge wads of cash.

We can't say for sure that this entertainment center *was hurt by the loss of Enrob executive clientele, but we wouldn't be surprised. All we can say is, we hope the whistleblowers are satisfied.*

AH, MEMORIES...

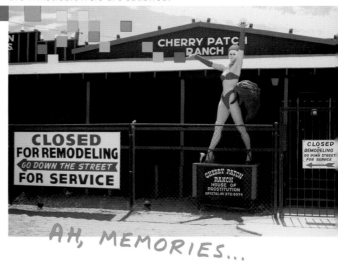

WHO DOES WHAT (OR USED TO) IN ENROB'S U.S. COMMAND CENTER

HEY, WHO CAME UP WITH THIS CHART? IT'S MUCH TOO ACCURATE.

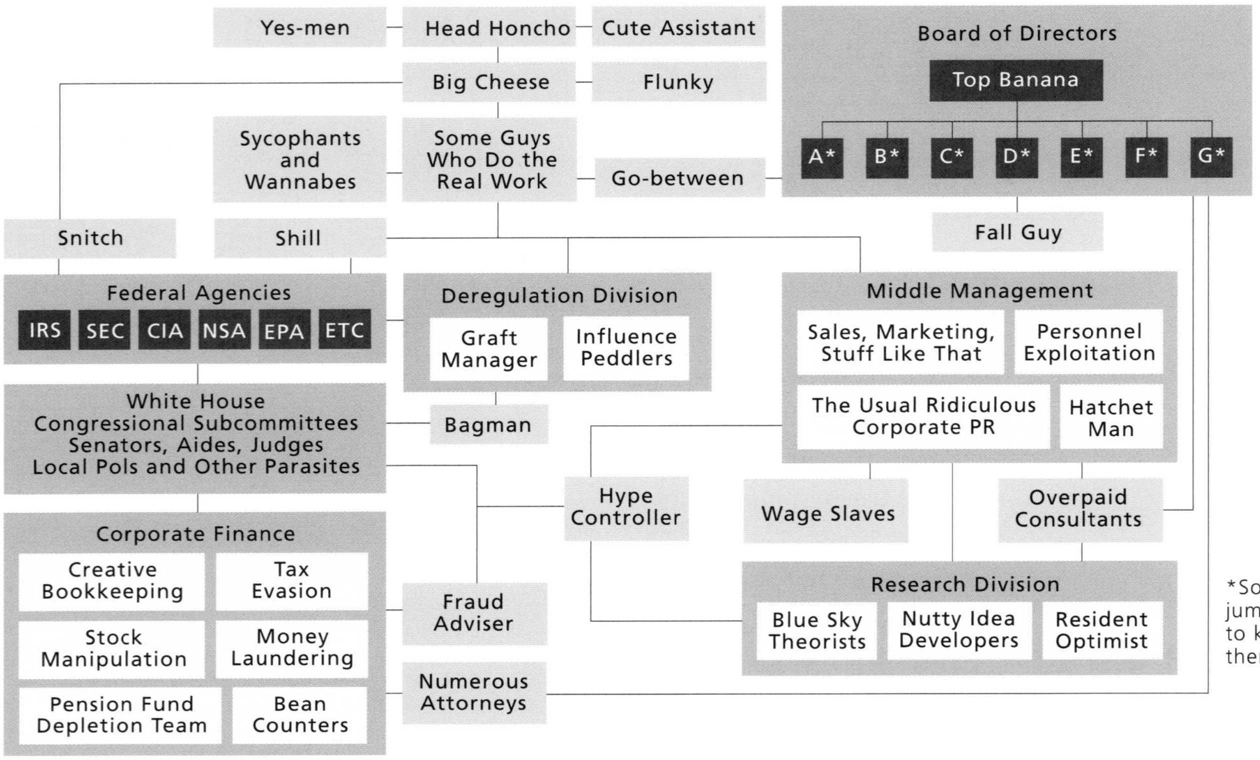
Yes-men
Head Honcho
Cute Assistant
Board of Directors
Top Banana
A*
B*
C*
D*
E*
F*
G*
Big Cheese
Flunky
Sycophants and Wannabes
Some Guys Who Do the Real Work
Go-between
Fall Guy
Snitch
Shill
Federal Agencies
IRS
SEC
CIA
NSA
EPA
ETC
Deregulation Division
Graft Manager
Influence Peddlers
Middle Management
Sales, Marketing, Stuff Like That
Personnel Exploitation
The Usual Ridiculous Corporate PR
Hatchet Man
White House
Congressional Subcommittees
Senators, Aides, Judges
Local Pols and Other Parasites
Bagman
Hype Controller
Wage Slaves
Overpaid Consultants
Corporate Finance
Creative Bookkeeping
Tax Evasion
Stock Manipulation
Money Laundering
Pension Fund Depletion Team
Bean Counters
Fraud Adviser
Numerous Attorneys
Research Division
Blue Sky Theorists
Nutty Idea Developers
Resident Optimist

*So many direc
jumping ship, h
to keep track o
them right now

Organization chart *shows the approximate interdepartmental relationships and job titles at Enrob. Formal titles and names have been omitted because of rapid personnel changes caused by opportunistic federal interventions, temporarily destabilizing our command structure.*

I'll have it redrawn with the more usual euphemisms substituted.

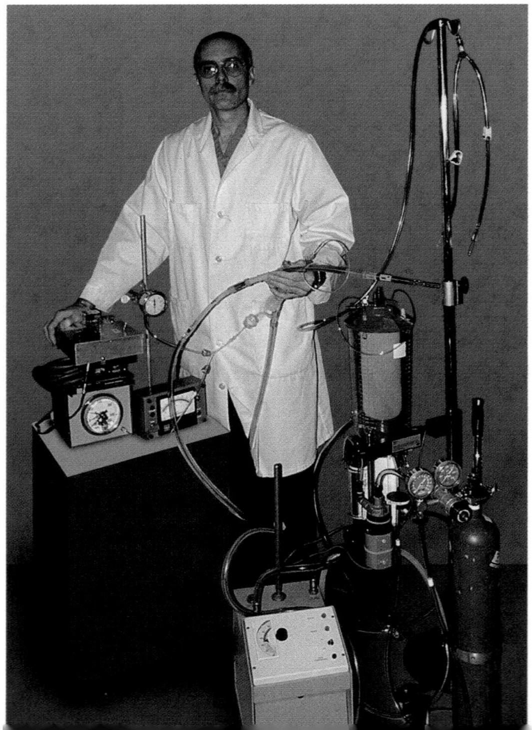

Waldo Zimmerman of Enrob's Special Projects Division *demonstrates his prototype for verifying employee loyalty. After a few "bad apples" betrayed our trust, we made a policy decision that anyone seeking an executive position will have to undergo Dr. Zimmerman's verification test. Doses of nitrous oxide alternating with painful electric shocks will quickly unmask anticorporate agitators who harbor an irrational grudge against free-market visionaries.*

Yeah, zap those anticorporate creeps, Waldo.

STATEMENT BY AUDITORS VALIDATES ENROB'S UNUSUAL BUSINESS PRACTICES, GENERALLY SPEAKING

Here at Absolutely Honest Auditors, LLC, we can say with complete confidence that when we add up the numbers twice, we get the same result both times.

That's about as far as we're willing to commit ourselves right now. The trouble is, corporate finances have gotten so complicated, no one really knows what's going on—so don't blame us if we end up scratching our heads. We do our best—okay? We look at a company's books, and if there's nothing obviously wrong, we say, "It looks to us as if there is nothing obviously wrong." That should be good enough. After all, Enrob's bookkeepers are smart cookies; we figure they have their bases covered. So why ask a bunch of annoying, nosy questions?

Sly Grubb, CEO of Absolutely Honest Auditors, LLC, makes a best-effort attempt to decipher the byzantine accounting practices of Enrob Corporation, prior to his indictment on grounds of willful negligence aggravated by an alcohol-induced stupor that had lasted for many years.

The above statement should not be construed as a warranty expressed or implied. If you think that this certification constitutes a legally binding declaration, that's your problem. Whatever this certification seems to say, we reserve the right to claim that it says something completely different, because everyone knows that it all depends on what your definition of "is" is. If we are called upon to elaborate, explain, or justify any statement herein, our auditors may plead mental incompetence or flee the country, because we really hate quibbling over picky little details.

Disclaimer: The signatory of this certification is not employed by Enrob, is not a stockholder in Enrob (although his wife owns a few million shares), and has not been bribed to make this statement. Well, he did receive a free vacation in Tasmania and a ten-percent-off coupon for his next purchase of home heating oil. But he has too much integrity to be influenced by little perks like that. At least, he's pretty sure he wasn't influenced. Not substantially, anyway.

Sworn without prejudice to the right to deny everything and blame someone else:

—Sly Grubb, Defrocked Public Accountant (retired)

I WISH WE COULD HAVE A MORE OUTSPOKEN STATEMENT. CAN WE REACH SLY IN FEDERAL PRISON?

31
Enrob

We all knew he was a lush. But let's not admit that we knew. Liability, you know?

It's a bit late to worry about that.

A SPECIAL MESSAGE FROM THE CHAIRMAN

Normally I would close this report with a frank assessment of our glorious company and its incredibly exciting future. Unfortunately I have been advised by our in-house legal team to seek protection from self-incrimination under the Fifth Amendment.

This disappoints me as much as it must disappoint you, but I'm sure this little problem will soon blow over, and Enrob can return to "market dominance as usual." Meanwhile, take it easy, watch your back, and have a nice day!

✗

—(name withheld),
Chairman of the Board,
Enrob Corporation

Former CEO Gus Grabbitt II leaves Enrob with a tragically small portion of the compensation that was rightfully his.

We love you, Gus! Sorry I don't have any spare change for your defense fund. I need it for mine!

F*** THE FEDS!

This is what we get for $42.5 million in political donations? We trusted those bastards! That was our biggest mistake.

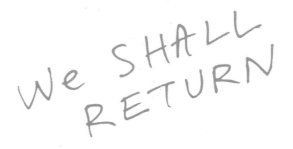

Here's the serious stuff:

Cover design and interior design by Erico Narita. Text by Charles Platt. Idea by John Silbersack. Photoshop collages and image editing by Charles Platt and Erico Narita. Charts, graphs, and 3D modeling by Charles Platt.

Special thanks: To Henry Beard and Gwyneth Cravens for refining the concept, and the staff of ReganBooks for their encouragement and enthusiasm.

Photo Credits: All photographs by Charles Platt except for falling man on front cover, inverted man on inside front cover, invisible man on page 18, masked man on page 25, and handcuffed man on page 32, by Erico Narita; Stock Exchange on front cover, pipes on front cover, brain on page 5, fiber on page 6, by Corbis Agency; man on page 1 by Lessley Anderson; Planet Mars on page 8 and Planet Earth on page 26 by NASA; woman on page 15 by Richard Kadrey; Al Capone on page 18 by FBI; cringing man on page 19 by Hyun Suk Song.

Weapons adviser: Joe Bready.

Geek memo: This project would have been impossible without Adobe Systems Incorporated, publishers of the world's finest software. We used only Adobe applications and typefaces to create this book. We also relied on: Olympus 3030-Z digital camera, Agfa and Polaroid scanners, GCC laser printer, Epson Stylus Photo ink-jet printer, Mac G4, iBook, and venerable PowerComputing PowerTower 144 with G3 accelerator card.

Political memo: Before denouncing illegalities perpetrated by unscrupulous entrepreneurs, one might consider that corrupt legislators are the enablers. The two species are codependent and equally culpable. Your elected representatives have additional details.

No similarity is intended between "Enrob" and any real corporation. The scenic photos are mislabeled for satirical purposes. All characters in this parody are fictitious and bear no intentional resemblance to any real person, living or dead.

ReganBooks

An Imprint of HarperCollins*Publishers*
www.reganbooks.com

USA $10.95
CANAD
ISBN 0-

*The Enro.......... Report is a parody
and should not be confused with
serious annual reports.*

ISBN 0-06-051896-0

51095 >

9 780060 518967

Endless Impossibilities. ™

Enrob Plaza
Enrob City, TX 00000
www.enrobreport.com

ENROB